WALK
in the
SPIRIT

Compiled by Bob Benoit

_____

Your Name

WALK **in the** SPIRIT

Compiled by Bob Benoit

Edited by Lisa Benoit

Photo by Mantas Hesthaven

© 2020 Bob Benoit

ISBN: 9798643350088

See JustheTruth.com

Amazon Kindle Direct Publishing (KDP) provides printing, distribution and ISBN services.

Contents

Overview

This is part four of a four-part series. The Apostle Paul writes in Galatians 5:25, "If we live in the Spirit, let us also walk in the Spirit?" How do we "*walk*" in the Spirit?" What is the difference between "*living*" and "*walking*" in the Spirit?

Scripture explains Scripture. So each lesson herein is a paragraph or two of scripture, in context, sorted by theme, where two or more of the words "*walk*", "*flesh*", and/or "*in the Spirit*" (and their various synonyms) appear in the same paragraph; followed by four questions. Each Scripture is in context, but it is best if you also read what surrounds these verses.

The following is a condensed summary of the Scriptures included in this Bible study on *walking in the Spirit*.

The Helper, the Holy Spirit teaches us all things. He makes intercession for us. He guides us in all Truth. He lives and dwells in us, in our heart. He helps us in our weakness. The peace of God rules in our hearts, the Word of Christ dwells richly in us. We hear His Word and are doers of the Word. We test the spirits to see if they are of God and understand what the will of the Lord is. We delight in the Lord. We abide and remain in the True Vine, in Christ and Him in us and His love in us. We are not alone. We are made alive together with Christ. We know that Jesus abides in us by the Spirit whom He has given us. We are found in Him and are being renewed by Him. We have been crucified with Christ. Our strength is *in Him*. We are more than conquerors through Him who loved us. We live by faith in the Son of God and nothing can separate us from God's love. We pray in the Holy Spirit.

To walk in the Spirit is to follow Jesus. We walk *in Him*. We walk *in the truth*. We are led by the Spirit. God directs our steps. We walk not by strength or might but by His Spirit, by

His grace. We walk in the newness of Life. We walk in the Light as children of light. We walk in the fruit of the Spirit. We walk in wisdom and understanding. We walk in the fear of the Lord and in the comfort of the Holy Spirit. We receive His correction. His commands are not burdensome. We walk by grace and His grace is sufficient. We speak the word of God with boldness and make disciples. Our hope is in Him and we trust Him with all our heart.

We walk the way in which He walked. We practice righteousness. We walk worthily of the calling with which we were called. We bear good fruit, are careful to maintain *good* works, and fight the good fight. We rejoice in hope, we rejoice in our sufferings. Whatever we do, we do it in the name of the Lord Jesus. We walk in humility and patience bearing with one another in love. We walk in love: we bear all things, believe all things, hope all things and endure all things. We give thanks in all things and give glory to God in the name of our Lord Jesus Christ.

We suggest you start by reading the Gospel message under the heading, Start Here. We cannot *walk in the Spirit* without knowing Jesus and responding to the Good News. Included herein is Appendix A - Small Group Facilitation Guide with step-by-step instructions to help homegroup and Bible study leaders host interactive meetings. Also, Appendix B – Sample Answers is given as an example of how one might answer the questions, particularly the first time.

Now, let us get ready to *walk in the Spirit*!

Start Here

We cannot *walk in the Spirit* without knowing and responding to the gospel of Jesus Christ. Here's a short form version – the gospel is about Jesus, who He is, what He's done, and why.

(1) **who Jesus Christ is** (the whole Bible points to who He is); Son of God, sent from heaven, Messiah, He was in the beginning, with God and was God, without sin, resurrected from the dead, our much-needed Savior, and *so much more*

(2) **what Jesus Christ has done**, particularly what He did on the cross: to take away your sins, to be your Savior, to reconcile you to God, to give you eternal life, to save you, to give you the Holy Spirit, and *so much more*

(3) **and why**, so that we might no longer live for ourselves, but for Him who died and rose again on our behalf, He is good, He is love. There is life in Christ Jesus, and *so much more*

He draws us to Himself; our part is to respond:

- to *repent* of our sins (change of heart, mind, and turn from old ways)

- to *believe* in Him with our heart (a continuum of faith, love, trust, and hope in Jesus Christ)

- to *confess* aloud that Jesus is LORD

- and to *follow* Him

Let us pray the prayer on the follow page together, out loud…

Our response to the calling of God (please pray out loud)

"Jesus, I believe You are Immanuel, God with us. I believe You came from Heaven, died on the Cross for *my sins*, and that you were resurrected from the dead. I confess that I have sinned and fallen short. I desire to leave my old life behind. I need a Savior to cleanse me of my sins, and that Savior is You, Jesus. Please forgive me and wash me." [pause]

"Thank You for what You've done on the Cross, thank You for everlasting life and the gift of the Holy Spirit. I receive your Spirit in my heart now." [pause]

"I look forward to my new journey – to know You better, love You, and follow You, now and forevermore, in Jesus name. Amen."

Baptism

WALK
in the
SPIRIT

#96 <u>John 15:1-5</u> (NASB)

"I am the true vine, and My Father is the vinedresser. [2] Every branch in Me that does not bear fruit, He takes away; and every *branch* that bears fruit, He prunes it so that it may bear more fruit. [3] You are already clean because of the word which I have spoken to you. [4] Abide in Me, and I in you. As the branch cannot bear fruit of itself unless it abides in the vine, so neither *can* you unless you abide in Me. [5] I am the vine, you are the branches; he who abides in Me and I in him, he bears much fruit, for apart from Me you can do nothing.

What insight if any does this Scripture give you about what it looks like to *walk in the Spirit*? [See Appendix B for sample answers if needed]

To *walk in the Spirit* we need to know the Spirit, Jesus, the Word. What words are used in this text to remind you of who Jesus/Spirit/God is?

What distractions are noted herein (if any) that might hinder someone from *walking in the Spirit*?

How can I apply this instruction to my life going forward, in my daily *walk in the Spirit*?

#97 Galatians 5:22-25 (NASB)

But the fruit of the Spirit is love, joy, peace, patience, kindness, goodness, faithfulness, ²³ gentleness, self-control; against such things there is no law. ²⁴ Now those who belong to Christ Jesus have crucified the flesh with its passions and desires. ²⁵ If we live by the Spirit, let us also walk by the Spirit. ²⁶ Let us not become boastful, challenging one another, envying one another.

What insight if any does this Scripture give you about what it looks like to *walk in the Spirit*? [See Appendix B for sample answers if needed]

To *walk in the Spirit* we need to know the Spirit, Jesus, the Word. What words are used in this text to remind you of who Jesus/Spirit/God is?

What distractions are noted herein (if any) that might hinder someone from *walking in the Spirit*?

How can I apply this instruction to my life going forward, in my daily *walk in the Spirit*?

#98 Luke 9:23-26 (see also Mark 8:34-38, Matthew 16:24-27)
He said to all, "If anyone desires to come after me, let him deny himself, take up his cross, and follow me. [24] For whoever desires to save his life will lose it, but whoever will lose his life for my sake, will save it. [25] For what does it profit a man if he gains the whole world, and loses or forfeits his own self? [26] For whoever will be ashamed of me and of my words, of him will the Son of Man be ashamed, when he comes in his glory, and the glory of the Father, and of the holy angels.

What insight if any does this Scripture give you about what it looks like to *walk in the Spirit*? [See Appendix B for sample answers if needed]

To *walk in the Spirit* we need to know the Spirit, Jesus, the Word. What words are used in this text to remind you of who Jesus/Spirit/God is?

What distractions are noted herein (if any) that might hinder someone from *walking in the Spirit*?

How can I apply this instruction to my life going forward, in my daily *walk in the Spirit*?

#99 Proverbs 3:5-13 (NASB)

Trust in the Lord with all your heart and do not lean on your own understanding. [6] In all your ways acknowledge Him, and He will make your paths straight. [7] Do not be wise in your own eyes; fear the Lord and turn away from evil. [8] It will be healing to your body and refreshment to your bones. [9] Honor the Lord from your wealth and from the first of all your produce; [10] So your barns will be filled with plenty and your vats will overflow with new wine. [11] My son, do not reject the discipline of the Lord or loathe His reproof, [12] For whom the Lord loves He reproves, even as a father *corrects* the son in whom he delights. [13] How blessed is the man who finds wisdom and the man who gains understanding.

What insight if any does this Scripture give you about what it looks like to *walk in the Spirit*?

To *walk in the Spirit* we need to know the Spirit, Jesus, the Word. What words are used in this text to remind you of who Jesus/Spirit/God is?

What distractions are noted herein (if any) that might hinder someone from *walking in the Spirit*?

How can I apply this instruction to my life going forward, in my daily *walk in the Spirit*?

#100 Psalm 37:1-11 (NASB)

Do not fret because of evildoers, be not envious toward wrongdoers. [2] For they will wither quickly like the grass and fade like the green herb. [3] Trust in the Lord and do good; dwell in the land and cultivate faithfulness. [4] Delight yourself in the Lord; and He will give you the desires of your heart. [5] Commit your way to the Lord, trust also in Him, and He will do it. [6] He will bring forth your righteousness as the light and your judgment as the noonday. [7] Rest in the Lord and wait patiently for Him; do not fret because of him who prospers in his way, because of the man who carries out wicked schemes. [8] Cease from anger and forsake wrath; do not fret; *it leads* only to evildoing. [9] For evildoers will be cut off, but those who wait for the Lord, they will inherit the land. [10] Yet a little while and the wicked man will be no more; and you will look carefully for his place and he will not be *there*. [11] But the humble will inherit the land and will delight themselves in abundant prosperity.

What insight if any does this Scripture give you about what it looks like to *walk in the Spirit*?

To *walk in the Spirit* we need to know the Spirit, Jesus, the Word. What words are used in this text to remind you of who Jesus/Spirit/God is?

What distractions are noted herein (if any) that might hinder someone from *walking in the Spirit*?

How can I apply this instruction to my life going forward, in my daily *walk in the Spirit*?

#101 Galatians 5:13-17 ^(NASB)

For you were called to freedom, brethren; only *do* not *turn* your freedom into an opportunity for the flesh, but through love serve one another. ¹⁴ For the whole Law is fulfilled in one word, in the *statement*, "You shall love your neighbor as yourself." ¹⁵ But if you bite and devour one another, take care that you are not consumed by one another. ¹⁶ But I say, walk by the Spirit, and you will not carry out the desire of the flesh. ¹⁷ For the flesh sets its desire against the Spirit, and the Spirit against the flesh; for these are in opposition to one another, so that you may not do the things that you please.

What insight if any does this Scripture give you about what it looks like to *walk in the Spirit*?

To *walk in the Spirit* we need to know the Spirit, Jesus, the Word. What words are used in this text to remind you of who Jesus/Spirit/God is?

What distractions are noted herein (if any) that might hinder someone from *walking in the Spirit*?

How can I apply this instruction to my life going forward, in my daily *walk in the Spirit*?

#102 Galatians 5:18-21 ^(NASB)

But if you are led by the Spirit, you are not under the Law. ¹⁹ Now the deeds of the flesh are evident, which are: immorality, impurity, sensuality, ²⁰ idolatry, sorcery, enmities, strife, jealousy, outbursts of anger, disputes, dissensions, factions, ²¹ envying, drunkenness, carousing, and things like these, of which I forewarn you, just as I have forewarned you, that those who practice such things will not inherit the kingdom of God.

What insight if any does this Scripture give you about what it looks like to *walk in the Spirit*?

To *walk in the Spirit* we need to know the Spirit, Jesus, the Word. What words are used in this text to remind you of who Jesus/Spirit/God is?

What distractions are noted herein (if any) that might hinder someone from *walking in the Spirit*?

How can I apply this instruction to my life going forward, in my daily *walk in the Spirit*?

#103 Colossians 2:4-10 ^(NASB)

I say this so that no one will delude you with persuasive argument. [5] For even though I am absent in body, nevertheless I am with you in spirit, rejoicing to see your good discipline and the stability of your faith in Christ. [6] Therefore as you have received Christ Jesus the Lord, *so* walk in Him, [7] having been firmly rooted *and now* being built up in Him and established in your faith, just as you were instructed, *and* overflowing with gratitude. [8] See to it that no one takes you captive through philosophy and empty deception, according to the tradition of men, according to the elementary principles of the world, rather than according to Christ. [9] For in Him all the fullness of Deity dwells in bodily form, [10] and in Him you have been made complete, and He is the head over all rule and authority;

What insight if any does this Scripture give you about what it looks like to *walk in the Spirit*?

To *walk in the Spirit* we need to know the Spirit, Jesus, the Word. What words are used in this text to remind you of who Jesus/Spirit/God is?

What distractions are noted herein (if any) that might hinder someone from *walking in the Spirit*?

How can I apply this instruction to my life going forward, in my daily *walk in the Spirit*?

#104 1 John 2:1-6 (ESV)

My little children, I am writing these things to you so that you may not sin. But if anyone does sin, we have an advocate with the Father, Jesus Christ the righteous. [2] He is the propitiation for our sins, and not for ours only but also for the sins of the whole world. [3] And by this we know that we have come to know him, if we keep his commandments. [4] Whoever says "I know him" but does not keep his commandments is a liar, and the truth is not in him, [5] but whoever keeps his word, in him truly the love of God is perfected. By this we may know that we are in him: [6] whoever says he abides in him ought to walk in the same way in which he walked.

What insight if any does this Scripture give you about what it looks like to *walk in the Spirit*?

To *walk in the Spirit* we need to know the Spirit, Jesus, the Word. What words are used in this text to remind you of who Jesus/Spirit/God is?

What distractions are noted herein (if any) that might hinder someone from *walking in the Spirit*?

How can I apply this instruction to my life going forward, in my daily *walk in the Spirit*?

#105 1 John 1:4-10 (NASB)

These things we write, so that our joy may be made complete. [5] This is the message we have heard from Him and announce to you, that God is Light, and in Him there is no darkness at all. [6] If we say that we have fellowship with Him and *yet* walk in the darkness, we lie and do not practice the truth; [7] but if we walk in the Light as He Himself is in the Light, we have fellowship with one another, and the blood of Jesus His Son cleanses us from all sin. [8] If we say that we have no sin, we are deceiving ourselves and the truth is not in us. [9] If we confess our sins, He is faithful and righteous to forgive us our sins and to cleanse us from all unrighteousness. [10] If we say that we have not sinned, we make Him a liar and His word is not in us.

What insight if any does this Scripture give you about what it looks like to *walk in the Spirit*?

To *walk in the Spirit* we need to know the Spirit, Jesus, the Word. What words are used in this text to remind you of who Jesus/Spirit/God is?

What distractions are noted herein (if any) that might hinder someone from *walking in the Spirit*?

How can I apply this instruction to my life going forward, in my daily *walk in the Spirit*?

#106 Romans 6:1-6

What shall we say then? Shall we continue in sin, that grace may abound? [2] May it never be! We who died to sin, how could we live in it any longer? [3] Or don't you know that all we who were baptized into Christ Jesus were baptized into his death? [4] We were buried therefore with him through baptism into death, that just as Christ was raised from the dead through the glory of the Father, so we also might walk in newness of life. [5] For if we have become united with him in the likeness of his death, we will also be part of his resurrection; [6] knowing this, that our old man was crucified with him, that the body of sin might be done away with, so that we would no longer be in bondage to sin.

What insight if any does this Scripture give you about what it looks like to *walk in the Spirit*?

To *walk in the Spirit* we need to know the Spirit, Jesus, the Word. What words are used in this text to remind you of who Jesus/Spirit/God is?

What distractions are noted herein (if any) that might hinder someone from *walking in the Spirit*?

How can I apply this instruction to my life going forward, in my daily *walk in the Spirit*?

#107 John 16:7-15

Nevertheless I tell you the truth. It is to your advantage that I go away; for if I do not go away, the Helper will not come to you; but if I depart, I will send Him to you. [8] And when He has come, He will convict the world of sin, and of righteousness, and of judgment: [9] of sin, because they do not believe in Me; [10] of righteousness, because I go to My Father and you see Me no more; [11] of judgment, because the ruler of this world is judged. [12] "I still have many things to say to you, but you cannot bear *them* now. [13] However, when He, the Spirit of truth, has come, He will guide you into all truth; for He will not speak on His own *authority,* but whatever He hears He will speak; and He will tell you things to come. [14] He will glorify Me, for He will take of what is Mine and declare *it* to you. [15] All things that the Father has are Mine. Therefore I said that He will take of Mine and declare *it* to you.

What insight if any does this Scripture give you about what it looks like to *walk in the Spirit*?

To *walk in the Spirit* we need to know the Spirit, Jesus, the Word. What words are used in this text to remind you of who Jesus/Spirit/God is?

What distractions are noted herein (if any) that might hinder someone from *walking in the Spirit*?

How can I apply this instruction to my life going forward, in my daily *walk in the Spirit*?

#108 <u>James 3:13-18</u>

Who is wise and understanding among you? Let him show by his good conduct that his deeds are done in gentleness of wisdom. [14] But if you have bitter jealousy and selfish ambition in your heart, don't boast and don't lie against the truth. [15] This wisdom is not that which comes down from above, but is earthly, sensual, and demonic. [16] For where jealousy and selfish ambition are, there is confusion and every evil deed. [17] But <u>the wisdom that is from above is first pure, then peaceful, gentle, reasonable, full of mercy and good fruits, without partiality, and without hypocrisy.</u> [18] Now the <u>fruit of righteousness</u> <u>is sown in peace by those who make peace.</u>

What insight if any does this Scripture give you about what it looks like to *walk in the Spirit?*

To *walk in the Spirit* we need to know the Spirit, Jesus, the Word. What words are used in this text to remind you of who Jesus/Spirit/God is?

What distractions are noted herein (if any) that might hinder someone from *walking in the Spirit*?

How can I apply this instruction to my life going forward, in my daily *walk in the Spirit*?

#109 <u>1 John 3:18-24</u> ^(NASB)

Little children, let us not love with word or with tongue, but in deed and truth. ¹⁹ We will know by this that we are of the truth, and will assure our heart before Him ²⁰ in whatever our heart condemns us; for God is greater than our heart and knows all things. ²¹ Beloved, if our heart does not condemn us, we have confidence before God; ²² and whatever we ask we receive from Him, because we keep His commandments and do the things that are pleasing in His sight. ²³ This is His commandment, that <u>we believe in the name of His Son Jesus Christ, and love one another, just as He commanded us.</u> ²⁴ <u>The one who keeps His commandments abides in Him, and He in him. We know by this that He abides in us, by the Spirit</u> whom He has given us.

What insight if any does this Scripture give you about what it looks like to *walk in the Spirit*?

To *walk in the Spirit* we need to know the Spirit, Jesus, the Word. What words are used in this text to remind you of who Jesus/Spirit/God is?

What distractions are noted herein (if any) that might hinder someone from *walking in the Spirit*?

How can I apply this instruction to my life going forward, in my daily *walk in the Spirit*?

#110 Colossians 3:14-17

Above all these things, walk in love, which is the bond of perfection. [15] And let the peace of God rule in your hearts, to which also you were called in one body, and be thankful. [16] Let the word of Christ dwell in you richly; in all wisdom teaching and admonishing one another with psalms, hymns, and spiritual songs, singing with grace in your heart to the Lord. [17] Whatever you do, in word or in deed, do all in the name of the Lord Jesus, giving thanks to God the Father, through him.

What insight if any does this Scripture give you about what it looks like to *walk in the Spirit*?

To *walk in the Spirit* we need to know the Spirit, Jesus, the Word. What words are used in this text to remind you of who Jesus/Spirit/God is?

What distractions are noted herein (if any) that might hinder someone from *walking in the Spirit*?

How can I apply this instruction to my life going forward, in my daily *walk in the Spirit*?

#111 Isaiah 11:1-5 ^(NKJV)

There shall come forth a Rod from the stem of Jesse, and a Branch shall grow out of his roots. ² The Spirit of the Lord shall rest upon Him, the Spirit of wisdom and understanding, the Spirit of counsel and might, the Spirit of knowledge and of the fear of the Lord. ³ His delight *is* in the fear of the Lord, And He shall not judge by the sight of His eyes, nor decide by the hearing of His ears; ⁴ but with righteousness He shall judge the poor, and decide with equity for the meek of the earth; He shall strike the earth with the rod of His mouth, and with the breath of His lips He shall slay the wicked. ⁵ Righteousness shall be the belt of His loins, and faithfulness the belt of His waist.

What insight if any does this Scripture give you about what it looks like to *walk in the Spirit*?

To *walk in the Spirit* we need to know the Spirit, Jesus, the Word. What words are used in this text to remind you of who Jesus/Spirit/God is?

What distractions are noted herein (if any) that might hinder someone from *walking in the Spirit*?

How can I apply this instruction to my life going forward, in my daily *walk in the Spirit*?

#112 <u>Acts 9:31</u>

So the assemblies throughout all Judea, Galilee, and Samaria had <u>peace, and were built up. They were multiplied, walking in the fear of the Lord and in the comfort of the Holy Spirit</u>.

What insight if any does this Scripture give you about what it looks like to *walk in the Spirit*?

To *walk in the Spirit* we need to know the Spirit, Jesus, the Word. What words are used in this text to remind you of who Jesus/Spirit/God is?

What distractions are noted herein (if any) that might hinder someone from *walking in the Spirit*?

How can I apply this instruction to my life going forward, in my daily *walk in the Spirit*?

#113 1 John 3:7-10 (NASB)

Little children, make sure no one deceives you; the one who practices righteousness is righteous, just as He is righteous; [8] the one who practices sin is of the devil; for the devil has sinned from the beginning. The Son of God appeared for this purpose, to destroy the works of the devil. [9] No one who is born of God practices sin, because His seed abides in him; and he cannot sin, because he is born of God. [10] By this the children of God and the children of the devil are obvious: anyone who does not practice righteousness is not of God, nor the one who does not love his brother.

What insight if any does this Scripture give you about what it looks like to *walk in the Spirit*?

To *walk in the Spirit* we need to know the Spirit, Jesus, the Word. What words are used in this text to remind you of who Jesus/Spirit/God is?

What distractions are noted herein (if any) that might hinder someone from *walking in the Spirit*?

How can I apply this instruction to my life going forward, in my daily *walk in the Spirit*?

#114 Ephesians 4:1-7

I therefore, the prisoner in the Lord, beg you to walk worthily of the calling with which you were called, ² with all lowliness and humility, with patience, bearing with one another in love, ³ being eager to keep the unity of the Spirit in the bond of peace. ⁴ There is one body and one Spirit, even as you also were called in one hope of your calling, ⁵ one Lord, one faith, one baptism, ⁶ one God and Father of all, who is over all and through all, and in us all. ⁷ But to each one of us, the grace was given according to the measure of the gift of Christ.

What insight if any does this Scripture give you about what it looks like to *walk in the Spirit*?

To *walk in the Spirit* we need to know the Spirit, Jesus, the Word. What words are used in this text to remind you of who Jesus/Spirit/God is?

What distractions are noted herein (if any) that might hinder someone from *walking in the Spirit*?

How can I apply this instruction to my life going forward, in my daily *walk in the Spirit*?

#115 Ephesians 5:1-7

Be therefore imitators of God, as beloved children. [2] Walk in love, even as Christ also loved us and gave himself up for us, an offering and a sacrifice to God for a sweet-smelling fragrance. [3] But sexual immorality, and all uncleanness or covetousness, let it not even be mentioned among you, as becomes saints; [4] nor filthiness, nor foolish talking, nor jesting, which are not appropriate, but rather giving of thanks. [5] Know this for sure, that no sexually immoral person, nor unclean person, nor covetous man, who is an idolater, has any inheritance in the Kingdom of Christ and God. [6] Let no one deceive you with empty words. For because of these things, the wrath of God comes on the children of disobedience. [7] Therefore don't be partakers with them.

What insight if any does this Scripture give you about what it looks like to *walk in the Spirit*?

To *walk in the Spirit* we need to know the Spirit, Jesus, the Word. What words are used in this text to remind you of who Jesus/Spirit/God is?

What distractions are noted herein (if any) that might hinder someone from *walking in the Spirit*?

How can I apply this instruction to my life going forward, in my daily *walk in the Spirit*?

#116 Ephesians 5:8-14

For you were once darkness, but are now light in the Lord. Walk as children of light, ⁹ for the fruit of the Spirit is in all goodness and righteousness and truth, ¹⁰ proving what is well pleasing to the Lord. ¹¹ Have no fellowship with the unfruitful deeds of darkness, but rather even reprove them. ¹² For it is a shame even to speak of the things which are done by them in secret. ¹³ But all things, when they are reproved, are revealed by the light, for everything that reveals is light. ¹⁴ Therefore he says, "Awake, you who sleep, and arise from the dead, and Christ will shine on you."

What insight if any does this Scripture give you about what it looks like to *walk in the Spirit*?

To *walk in the Spirit* we need to know the Spirit, Jesus, the Word. What words are used in this text to remind you of who Jesus/Spirit/God is?

What distractions are noted herein (if any) that might hinder someone from *walking in the Spirit*?

How can I apply this instruction to my life going forward, in my daily *walk in the Spirit*?

#117 Ephesians 5:15-21

Therefore watch carefully how you walk, not as unwise, but as wise, ¹⁶ redeeming the time, because the days are evil. ¹⁷ Therefore don't be foolish, but understand what the will of the Lord is. ¹⁸ Don't be drunken with wine, in which is dissipation, but be filled with the Spirit, ¹⁹ speaking to one another in psalms, hymns, and spiritual songs; singing and making melody in your heart to the Lord; ²⁰ giving thanks always concerning all things in the name of our Lord Jesus Christ, to God, even the Father; ²¹ subjecting yourselves to one another in the fear of Christ.

What insight if any does this Scripture give you about what it looks like to *walk in the Spirit*?

To *walk in the Spirit* we need to know the Spirit, Jesus, the Word. What words are used in this text to remind you of who Jesus/Spirit/God is?

What distractions are noted herein (if any) that might hinder someone from *walking in the Spirit*?

How can I apply this instruction to my life going forward, in my daily *walk in the Spirit*?

#118 2 Corinthians 12:7-10

By reason of the exceeding greatness of the revelations, that I should not be exalted excessively, a thorn in the flesh was given to me: a messenger of Satan to torment me, that I should not be exalted excessively. [8] Concerning this thing, I begged the Lord three times that it might depart from me. [9] He has said to me, "My grace is sufficient for you, for my power is made perfect in weakness." Most gladly therefore I will rather glory in my weaknesses, that the power of Christ may rest on me. [10] Therefore I take pleasure in weaknesses, in injuries, in necessities, in persecutions, and in distresses, for Christ's sake. For when I am weak, then am I strong.

What insight if any does this Scripture give you about what it looks like to *walk in the Spirit*?

To *walk in the Spirit* we need to know the Spirit, Jesus, the Word. What words are used in this text to remind you of who Jesus/Spirit/God is?

What distractions are noted herein (if any) that might hinder someone from *walking in the Spirit*?

How can I apply this instruction to my life going forward, in my daily *walk in the Spirit*?

#119 1 John 4:1-6

Beloved, don't believe every spirit, but test the spirits, whether they are of God, because many false prophets have gone out into the world. [2] By this you know the Spirit of God: every spirit who confesses that Jesus Christ has come in the flesh is of God, [3] and every spirit who doesn't confess that Jesus Christ has come in the flesh is not of God, and this is the spirit of the Antichrist, of whom you have heard that it comes. Now it is in the world already. [4] You are of God, little children, and have overcome them; because greater is he who is in you than he who is in the world. [5] They are of the world. Therefore they speak of the world, and the world hears them. [6] We are of God. He who knows God listens to us. He who is not of God doesn't listen to us. By this we know the spirit of truth, and the spirit of error.

What insight if any does this Scripture give you about what it looks like to *walk in the Spirit*?

To *walk in the Spirit* we need to know the Spirit, Jesus, the Word. What words are used in this text to remind you of who Jesus/Spirit/God is?

What distractions are noted herein (if any) that might hinder someone from *walking in the Spirit*?

How can I apply this instruction to my life going forward, in my daily *walk in the Spirit*?

#120 <u>Matthew 28:16-20</u> ^(NKJV)

But the eleven disciples went into Galilee, to the mountain where Jesus had sent them. ¹⁷ When they saw him, they bowed down to him; but some doubted. ¹⁸ Jesus came to them and spoke to them, saying, "<u>All authority has been given to me in heaven and on earth.</u> ¹⁹ <u>Go and make disciples of all nations, baptizing them in the name of the Father and of the Son and of the Holy Spirit,</u> ²⁰ <u>teaching them to observe all things that I commanded you. Behold, I am with you always, even to the end of the age.</u>" Amen.

What insight if any does this Scripture give you about what it looks like to *walk in the Spirit*?

To *walk in the Spirit* we need to know the Spirit, Jesus, the Word. What words are used in this text to remind you of who Jesus/Spirit/God is?

What distractions are noted herein (if any) that might hinder someone from *walking in the Spirit*?

How can I apply this instruction to my life going forward, in my daily *walk in the Spirit*?

#121 Luke 6:43-49 also see Matthew 12:33-37 (ESV)

"For no good tree bears bad fruit, nor again does a bad tree bear good fruit, [44] for each tree is known by its own fruit. For figs are not gathered from thornbushes, nor are grapes picked from a bramble bush. [45] The good person out of the good treasure of his heart produces good, and the evil person out of his evil treasure produces evil, for out of the abundance of the heart his mouth speaks. [46] "Why do you call me 'Lord, Lord,' and not do what I tell you? [47] Everyone who comes to me and hears my words and does them, I will show you what he is like: [48] he is like a man building a house, who dug deep and laid the foundation on the rock. And when a flood arose, the stream broke against that house and could not shake it, because it had been well built. [49] But the one who hears and does not do them is like a man who built a house on the ground without a foundation. When the stream broke against it, immediately it fell, and the ruin of that house was great."

What insight if any does this Scripture give you about what it looks like to *walk in the Spirit*?

To *walk in the Spirit* we need to know the Spirit, Jesus, the Word. What words are used in this text to remind you of who Jesus/Spirit/God is?

What distractions are noted herein (if any) that might hinder someone from *walking in the Spirit*?

How can I apply this instruction to my life going forward, in my daily *walk in the Spirit*?

#122 James 1:19-25

So, then, my beloved brothers, let every man be swift to hear, slow to speak, and slow to anger; [20] for the anger of man doesn't produce the righteousness of God. [21] Therefore, putting away all filthiness and overflowing of wickedness, receive with humility the implanted word, which is able to save your souls. [22] But be doers of the word, and not only hearers, deluding your own selves. [23] For if anyone is a hearer of the word and not a doer, he is like a man looking at his natural face in a mirror; [24] for he sees himself, and goes away, and immediately forgets what kind of man he was. [25] But he who looks into the perfect law of freedom and continues, not being a hearer who forgets, but a doer of the work, this man will be blessed in what he does.

What insight if any does this Scripture give you about what it looks like to *walk in the Spirit*?

To *walk in the Spirit* we need to know the Spirit, Jesus, the Word. What words are used in this text to remind you of who Jesus/Spirit/God is?

What distractions are noted herein (if any) that might hinder someone from *walking in the Spirit*?

How can I apply this instruction to my life going forward, in my daily *walk in the Spirit*?

#123 Galatians 2:15-21

"We, being Jews by nature, and not Gentile sinners, [16] yet knowing that a man is not justified by the works of the law but through faith in Jesus Christ, even we believed in Christ Jesus, that we might be justified by faith in Christ, and not by the works of the law, because no flesh will be justified by the works of the law. [17] But if while we sought to be justified in Christ, we ourselves also were found sinners, is Christ a servant of sin? Certainly not! [18] For if I build up again those things which I destroyed, I prove myself a law-breaker. [19] For I, through the law, died to the law, that I might live to God. [20] I have been crucified with Christ, and it is no longer I who live, but Christ lives in me. That life which I now live in the flesh, I live by faith in the Son of God, who loved me, and gave himself up for me. [21] I don't reject the grace of God. For if righteousness is through the law, then Christ died for nothing!"

What insight if any does this Scripture give you about what it looks like to *walk in the Spirit*?

To *walk in the Spirit* we need to know the Spirit, Jesus, the Word. What words are used in this text to remind you of who Jesus/Spirit/God is?

What distractions are noted herein (if any) that might hinder someone from *walking in the Spirit*?

How can I apply this instruction to my life going forward, in my daily *walk in the Spirit*?

#124 Psalm 84:5-12

Blessed are those whose strength is in you, who have set their hearts on a pilgrimage. [6] Passing through the valley of Weeping, they make it a place of springs. Yes, the autumn rain covers it with blessings. [7] They go from strength to strength. Every one of them appears before God in Zion. [8] Yahweh, God of Armies, hear my prayer. Listen, God of Jacob. Selah. [9] Behold, God our shield, look at the face of your anointed. [10] For a day in your courts is better than a thousand. I would rather be a doorkeeper in the house of my God, than to dwell in the tents of wickedness. [11] For Yahweh God is a sun and a shield. Yahweh will give grace and glory. He withholds no good thing from those who walk blamelessly. [12] Yahweh of Armies, blessed is the man who trusts in you.

What insight if any does this Scripture give you about what it looks like to *walk in the Spirit*?

To *walk in the Spirit* we need to know the Spirit, Jesus, the Word. What words are used in this text to remind you of who Jesus/Spirit/God is?

What distractions are noted herein (if any) that might hinder someone from *walking in the Spirit*?

How can I apply this instruction to my life going forward, in my daily *walk in the Spirit*?

#125 Acts 7:51-60

"*You* stiff-necked and uncircumcised in heart and ears! You always resist the Holy Spirit; as your fathers *did,* so *do* you. [52] Which of the prophets did your fathers not persecute? And they killed those who foretold the coming of the Just One, of whom you now have become the betrayers and murderers, [53] who have received the law by the direction of angels and have not kept *it*." [54] When they heard these things they were cut to the heart, and they gnashed at him with *their* teeth. [55] But he, being full of the Holy Spirit, gazed into heaven and saw the glory of God, and Jesus standing at the right hand of God, [56] and said, "Look! I see the heavens opened and the Son of Man standing at the right hand of God!" [57] But they cried out with a loud voice and stopped their ears, then rushed at him with one accord. [58] They threw him out of the city and stoned him. The witnesses placed their garments at the feet of a young man named Saul. [59] They stoned Stephen as he called out, saying, "Lord Jesus, receive my spirit!" [60] He kneeled down, and cried with a loud voice, "Lord, don't hold this sin against them!" When he had said this, he fell asleep.

What insight if any does this Scripture give you about what it looks like to *walk in the Spirit*?

To *walk in the Spirit* we need to know the Spirit, Jesus, the Word. What words are used in this text to remind you of who Jesus/Spirit/God is?

What distractions are noted herein (if any) that might hinder someone from *walking in the Spirit*?

How can I apply this instruction to my life going forward, in my daily *walk in the Spirit*?

#126 1 Timothy 1:12-19 (NASB)

I thank Christ Jesus our Lord, who has strengthened me, because He considered me faithful, putting me into service, [13] even though I was formerly a blasphemer and a persecutor and a violent aggressor. Yet I was shown mercy because I acted ignorantly in unbelief; [14] and the grace of our Lord was more than abundant, with the faith and love which are found in Christ Jesus. [15] It is a trustworthy statement, deserving full acceptance, that Christ Jesus came into the world to save sinners, among whom I am foremost of all. [16] Yet for this reason I found mercy, so that in me as the foremost, Jesus Christ might demonstrate His perfect patience as an example or those who would believe in Him for eternal life. [17] Now to the King eternal, immortal, invisible, the only God, *be* honor and glory forever and ever. Amen. [8] This command I entrust to you, Timothy, *my* son, in accordance with the prophecies previously made concerning you, that by them you fight the good fight, [19] keeping faith and a good conscience, which some have rejected and suffered shipwreck in regard to their faith.

What insight if any does this Scripture give you about what it looks like to *walk in the Spirit*?

To *walk in the Spirit* we need to know the Spirit, Jesus, the Word. What words are used in this text to remind you of who Jesus/Spirit/God is?

What distractions are noted herein (if any) that might hinder someone from *walking in the Spirit*?

How can I apply this instruction to my life going forward, in my daily *walk in the Spirit*?

#127 Zechariah 4:5-7

Then the angel who talked with me answered me, "Don't you know what these are?" I said, "No, my lord." [6] Then he answered and spoke to me, saying, "This is Yahweh's word to Zerubbabel, saying, 'Not by might, nor by power, but by my Spirit,' says Yahweh of Armies. [7] Who are you, great mountain? Before Zerubbabel you are a plain; and he will bring out the capstone with shouts of 'Grace, grace, to it!'"

What insight if any does this Scripture give you about what it looks like to *walk in the Spirit*?

To *walk in the Spirit* we need to know the Spirit, Jesus, the Word. What words are used in this text to remind you of who Jesus/Spirit/God is?

What distractions are noted herein (if any) that might hinder someone from *walking in the Spirit*?

How can I apply this instruction to my life going forward, in my daily *walk in the Spirit*?

#128 John 12:42-46

Nevertheless even many of the rulers believed in him, but because of the Pharisees they didn't confess it, so that they wouldn't be put out of the synagogue, [43] for they loved men's praise more than God's praise. [44] Jesus cried out and said, "Whoever believes in me, believes not in me, but in him who sent me. [45] He who sees me sees him who sent me. [46] I have come as a light into the world, that whoever believes in me may not remain in the darkness.

What insight if any does this Scripture give you about what it looks like to *walk in the Spirit?*

To *walk in the Spirit* we need to know the Spirit, Jesus, the Word. What words are used in this text to remind you of who Jesus/Spirit/God is?

What distractions are noted herein (if any) that might hinder someone from *walking in the Spirit*?

How can I apply this instruction to my life going forward, in my daily *walk in the Spirit*?

#129 Philippians 3:8-14

Yes most certainly, and I count all things to be a loss for the excellency of the knowledge of Christ Jesus, my Lord, for whom I suffered the loss of all things, and count them nothing but refuse, that I may gain Christ [9] and be found in him, not having a righteousness of my own, that which is of the law, but that which is through faith in Christ, the righteousness which is from God by faith, [10] that I may know him, and the power of his resurrection, and the fellowship of his sufferings, becoming conformed to his death, [11] if by any means I may attain to the resurrection from the dead. [12] Not that I have already obtained, or am already made perfect; but I press on, that I may take hold of that for which also I was taken hold of by Christ Jesus. [13] Brothers, I don't regard myself as yet having taken hold, but one thing I do: forgetting the things which are behind, and stretching forward to the things which are before, [14] I press on toward the goal for the prize of the high calling of God in Christ Jesus.

What insight if any does this Scripture give you about what it looks like to *walk in the Spirit*?

To *walk in the Spirit* we need to know the Spirit, Jesus, the Word. What words are used in this text to remind you of who Jesus/Spirit/God is?

What distractions are noted herein (if any) that might hinder someone from *walking in the Spirit*?

How can I apply this instruction to my life going forward, in my daily *walk in the Spirit*?

#130 Titus 2:11-3:7

For the grace of God has appeared, bringing salvation to all men, [12] instructing us to the intent that, denying ungodliness and worldly lusts, we would live soberly, righteously, and godly in this present age; [13] looking for the blessed hope and appearing of the glory of our great God and Savior, Jesus Christ, [14] who gave himself for us, that he might redeem us from all iniquity, and purify for himself a people for his own possession, zealous for good works. [15] Say these things and exhort and reprove with all authority. Let no one despise you. [3:1] Remind them to be in subjection to rulers and to authorities, to be obedient, to be ready for every good work, [2] to speak evil of no one, not to be contentious, to be gentle, showing all humility toward all men. [3] For we were also once foolish, disobedient, deceived, serving various lusts and pleasures, living in malice and envy, hateful, and hating one another. [4] But when the kindness of God our Savior and his love toward mankind appeared, [5] not by works of righteousness which we did ourselves, but according to his mercy, he saved us through the washing of regeneration and renewing by the Holy Spirit, [6] whom he poured out on us richly, through Jesus Christ our Savior; [7] that being justified by his **grace**, we might be made heirs according to the hope of eternal life.

What insight if any does this Scripture give you about what it looks like to *walk in the Spirit*?

To *walk in the Spirit* we need to know the Spirit, Jesus, the Word. What words are used in this text to remind you of who Jesus/Spirit/God is?

What distractions are noted herein (if any) that might hinder someone from *walking in the Spirit*?

How can I apply this instruction to my life going forward, in my daily *walk in the Spirit*?

John 14:21-27 ^(NASB)

He who has My commandments and keeps them is the one who loves Me; and he who loves Me will be loved by My Father, and I will love him and will disclose Myself to him." ²² Judas (not Iscariot) *said to Him, "Lord, what then has happened that You are going to disclose Yourself to us and not to the world?" ²³ Jesus answered and said to him, "If anyone loves Me, he will keep My word; and My Father will love him, and We will come to him and make Our abode with him. ²⁴ He who does not love Me does not keep My words; and the word which you hear is not Mine, but the Father's who sent Me. ²⁵ "These things I have spoken to you while abiding with you. ²⁶ But the Helper, the Holy Spirit, whom the Father will send in My name, He will teach you all things, and bring to your remembrance all that I said to you. ²⁷ Peace I leave with you; My peace I give to you; not as the world gives do I give to you. Do not let your heart be troubled, nor let it be fearful.

What insight if any does this Scripture give you about what it looks like to *walk in the Spirit*?

To *walk in the Spirit* we need to know the Spirit, Jesus, the Word. What words are used in this text to remind you of who Jesus/Spirit/God is?

What distractions are noted herein (if any) that might hinder someone from *walking in the Spirit*?

How can I apply this instruction to my life going forward, in my daily *walk in the Spirit*?

#132 Ephesians 2:4-10

But God, being rich in mercy, for his great love with which he loved us, [5] even when we were dead through our trespasses, made us alive together with Christ—by grace you have been saved— [6] and raised us up with him, and made us to sit with him in the heavenly places in Christ Jesus, [7] that in the ages to come he might show the exceeding riches of his grace in kindness toward us in Christ Jesus; [8] for by grace you have been saved through faith, and that not of yourselves; it is the gift of God, [9] not of works, that no one would boast. [10] For we are his workmanship, created in Christ Jesus for good works, which God prepared before that we would walk in them.

What insight if any does this Scripture give you about what it looks like to *walk in the Spirit*?

To *walk in the Spirit* we need to know the Spirit, Jesus, the Word. What words are used in this text to remind you of who Jesus/Spirit/God is?

What distractions are noted herein (if any) that might hinder someone from *walking in the Spirit*?

How can I apply this instruction to my life going forward, in my daily *walk in the Spirit*?

#133 <u>Titus 3:4-9</u>

But when the kindness of God our Savior and his love toward mankind appeared, [5] not by works of righteousness which we did ourselves, but according to his mercy, he saved us through the washing of regeneration and renewing by the Holy Spirit, [6] whom he poured out on us richly, through Jesus Christ our Savior; [7] that <u>being justified by his grace, we might be made heirs according to the hope of eternal life.</u> [8] <u>This saying is faithful, and concerning these things I desire that you affirm confidently, so that those who have believed God may be careful to maintain good works. These things are good and profitable to men;</u> [9] but shun foolish questionings, genealogies, strife, and disputes about the law; for they are unprofitable and vain.

What insight if any does this Scripture give you about what it looks like to *walk in the Spirit*?

To *walk in the Spirit* we need to know the Spirit, Jesus, the Word. What words are used in this text to remind you of who Jesus/Spirit/God is?

What distractions are noted herein (if any) that might hinder someone from *walking in the Spirit*?

How can I apply this instruction to my life going forward, in my daily *walk in the Spirit*?

#134 <u>3 John 1-4</u> ^(NKJV)

The Elder, to the beloved Gaius, whom I love in truth: ² Beloved, I pray that you may prosper in all things and be in health, just as your soul prospers. ³ For <u>I rejoiced greatly when brethren came and testified of the truth *that is* in you, just as you walk in the truth.</u> ⁴ <u>I have no greater joy than to hear that my children walk in truth</u>.

What insight if any does this Scripture give you about what it looks like to *walk in the Spirit*?

To *walk in the Spirit* we need to know the Spirit, Jesus, the Word. What words are used in this text to remind you of who Jesus/Spirit/God is?

What distractions are noted herein (if any) that might hinder someone from *walking in the Spirit*?

How can I apply this instruction to my life going forward, in my daily *walk in the Spirit*?

#135 Galatians 3:1-7

Foolish Galatians, who has bewitched you not to obey the truth, before whose eyes Jesus Christ was openly portrayed among you as crucified? ² I just want to learn this from you: Did you receive the Spirit by the works of the law, or by hearing of faith? ³ Are you so foolish? Having begun in the Spirit, are you now completed in the flesh? ⁴ Did you suffer so many things in vain, if it is indeed in vain? ⁵ He therefore who supplies the Spirit to you and does miracles among you, does he do it by the works of the law, or by hearing of faith? ⁶ Even so, Abraham "believed God, and it was counted to him for righteousness." Genesis 15:6 ⁷ Know therefore that those who are of faith are children of Abraham.

What insight if any does this Scripture give you about what it looks like to *walk in the Spirit*?

To *walk in the Spirit* we need to know the Spirit, Jesus, the Word. What words are used in this text to remind you of who Jesus/Spirit/God is?

What distractions are noted herein (if any) that might hinder someone from *walking in the Spirit*?

How can I apply this instruction to my life going forward, in my daily *walk in the Spirit*?

#136 <u>Colossians 4:2-6</u>
<u>Continue steadfastly in prayer, watching in it with thanksgiving,</u>
<u>³ praying together for us also, that God may open to us a door for the</u>
<u>word, to speak the mystery of Christ, for which I am also in bonds, ⁴ that</u>
<u>I may reveal it as I ought to speak. ⁵ Walk in wisdom toward those who</u>
<u>are outside, redeeming the time. ⁶ Let your speech always be with grace,</u>
<u>seasoned with salt, that you may know how you ought to answer each</u>
<u>one</u>.

What insight if any does this Scripture give you about what it looks like
to *walk in the Spirit*?

To *walk in the Spirit* we need to know the Spirit, Jesus, the Word. What words are used in this text to remind you of who Jesus/Spirit/God is?

What distractions are noted herein (if any) that might hinder someone from *walking in the Spirit*?

How can I apply this instruction to my life going forward, in my daily *walk in the Spirit*?

#137 <u>Hebrews 10:19-25</u>

Having therefore, brothers, boldness to enter into the holy place by the blood of Jesus, [20] by the way which he dedicated for us, a new and living way, through the veil, that is to say, his flesh, [21] and <u>having a great priest over God's house,</u> [22] <u>let's draw near with a true heart in fullness of faith, having our hearts sprinkled from an evil conscience, and having our body washed with pure water,</u> [23] <u>let's hold fast the confession of our hope without wavering; for he who promised is faithful.</u> [24] <u>Let's consider how to provoke one another to love and good works,</u> [25] <u>not forsaking our own assembling together, as the custom of some is,</u> but exhorting one another, and so much the more as you see the Day approaching.

What insight if any does this Scripture give you about what it looks like to *walk in the Spirit*?

To *walk in the Spirit* we need to know the Spirit, Jesus, the Word. What words are used in this text to remind you of who Jesus/Spirit/God is?

What distractions are noted herein (if any) that might hinder someone from *walking in the Spirit*?

How can I apply this instruction to my life going forward, in my daily *walk in the Spirit*?

#138 <u>Matthew 10:18-22</u>

Yes, and you will be brought before governors and kings for my sake, for a testimony to them and to the nations. [19] But <u>when they deliver you up, don't be anxious how or what you will say, for it will be given you in that hour what you will say.</u> [20] <u>For it is not you who speak, but the Spirit of your Father who speaks in you.</u> [21] "Brother will deliver up brother to death, and the father his child. Children will rise up against parents and cause them to be put to death. [22] You will be hated by all men for my name's sake, but he who endures to the end will be saved.

What insight if any does this Scripture give you about what it looks like to *walk in the Spirit*?

To *walk in the Spirit* we need to know the Spirit, Jesus, the Word. What words are used in this text to remind you of who Jesus/Spirit/God is?

What distractions are noted herein (if any) that might hinder someone from *walking in the Spirit*?

How can I apply this instruction to my life going forward, in my daily *walk in the Spirit*?

#139 1 John 3:11-17 (NKJV)

For this is the message which you have heard from the beginning, that we should love one another; ¹² not as Cain, *who* was of the evil one and slew his brother. And for what reason did he slay him? Because his deeds were evil, and his brother's were righteous. ¹³ Do not be surprised, brethren, if the world hates you. ¹⁴ We know that we have passed out of death into life, because we love the brethren. He who does not love abides in death. ¹⁵ Everyone who hates his brother is a murderer; and you know that no murderer has eternal life abiding in him. ¹⁶ We know love by this, that He laid down His life for us; and we ought to lay down our lives for the brethren. ¹⁷ But whoever has the world's goods, and sees his brother in need and closes his heart against him, how does the love of God abide in him?

What insight if any does this Scripture give you about what it looks like to *walk in the Spirit*?

To *walk in the Spirit* we need to know the Spirit, Jesus, the Word. What words are used in this text to remind you of who Jesus/Spirit/God is?

What distractions are noted herein (if any) that might hinder someone from *walking in the Spirit*?

How can I apply this instruction to my life going forward, in my daily *walk in the Spirit*?

#140 1 Peter 1:22-25

Seeing you have purified your souls in your obedience to the truth through the Spirit in sincere brotherly affection, love one another from the heart fervently, ²³ having been born again, not of corruptible seed, but of incorruptible, through the word of God, which lives and remains forever. ²⁴ For, "All flesh is like gra-ss, and all of man's glory like the flower in the grass. The grass withers, and its flower falls; ²⁵ but the Lord's word endures forever." Isaiah 40:6-8 This is the word of Good News which was preached to you.

What insight if any does this Scripture give you about what it looks like to *walk in the Spirit*?

To *walk in the Spirit* we need to know the Spirit, Jesus, the Word. What words are used in this text to remind you of who Jesus/Spirit/God is?

What distractions are noted herein (if any) that might hinder someone from *walking in the Spirit*?

How can I apply this instruction to my life going forward, in my daily *walk in the Spirit*?

#141 1 John 2:7-11 (NASB)

Beloved, I am not writing a new commandment to you, but an old commandment which you have had from the beginning; the old commandment is the word which you have heard. [8] On the other hand, I am writing a new commandment to you, which is true in Him and in you, because the darkness is passing away and the true Light is already shining. [9] The one who says he is in the Light and *yet* hates his brother is in the darkness until now. [10] The one who loves his brother abides in the Light and there is no cause for stumbling in him. [11] But the one who hates his brother is in the darkness and walks in the darkness, and does not know where he is going because the darkness has blinded his eyes.

What insight if any does this Scripture give you about what it looks like to *walk in the Spirit*?

To *walk in the Spirit* we need to know the Spirit, Jesus, the Word. What words are used in this text to remind you of who Jesus/Spirit/God is?

What distractions are noted herein (if any) that might hinder someone from *walking in the Spirit*?

How can I apply this instruction to my life going forward, in my daily *walk in the Spirit*?

#142 2 Peter 1:5-9 (NASB)

Now for this very reason also, applying all diligence, in your faith supply moral excellence, and in *your* moral excellence, knowledge, [6] and in *your* knowledge, self-control, and in *your* self-control, perseverance, and in *your* perseverance, godliness, [7] and in *your* godliness, brotherly kindness, and in *your* brotherly kindness, love. [8] For if these *qualities* are yours and are increasing, they render you neither useless nor unfruitful in the true knowledge of our Lord Jesus Christ. [9] For he who lacks these *qualities* is blind *or* short-sighted, having forgotten *his* purification from his former sins.

What insight if any does this Scripture give you about what it looks like to *walk in the Spirit?*

To *walk in the Spirit* we need to know the Spirit, Jesus, the Word. What words are used in this text to remind you of who Jesus/Spirit/God is?

What distractions are noted herein (if any) that might hinder someone from *walking in the Spirit*?

How can I apply this instruction to my life going forward, in my daily *walk in the Spirit*?

#143 Romans 8:26-28

In the same way, the Spirit also helps our weaknesses, for we don't know how to pray as we ought. But the Spirit himself makes intercession for us with groanings which can't be uttered. [27] He who searches the hearts knows what is on the Spirit's mind, because he makes intercession for the saints according to God. [28] We know that all things work together for good for those who love God, for those who are called according to his purpose.

What insight if any does this Scripture give you about what it looks like to *walk in the Spirit?*

To *walk in the Spirit* we need to know the Spirit, Jesus, the Word. What words are used in this text to remind you of who Jesus/Spirit/God is?

What distractions are noted herein (if any) that might hinder someone from *walking in the Spirit*?

How can I apply this instruction to my life going forward, in my daily *walk in the Spirit*?

#144 Romans 8:35-39

Who shall separate us from the love of Christ? Could oppression, or anguish, or persecution, or famine, or nakedness, or peril, or sword? [36] Even as it is written, "For your sake we are killed all day long. We were accounted as sheep for the slaughter." Psalm 44:22 [37] No, in all these things, we are more than conquerors through him who loved us. [38] For I am persuaded that neither death, nor life, nor angels, nor principalities, nor things present, nor things to come, nor powers, [39] nor height, nor depth, nor any other created thing will be able to separate us from God's love which is in Christ Jesus our Lord.

What insight if any does this Scripture give you about what it looks like to *walk in the Spirit*?

To *walk in the Spirit* we need to know the Spirit, Jesus, the Word. What words are used in this text to remind you of who Jesus/Spirit/God is?

What distractions are noted herein (if any) that might hinder someone from *walking in the Spirit*?

How can I apply this instruction to my life going forward, in my daily *walk in the Spirit*?

#145 Jude 1:20-25

But you, beloved, keep building up yourselves on your most holy faith, praying in the Holy Spirit. [21] Keep yourselves in God's love, looking for the mercy of our Lord Jesus Christ to eternal life. [22] On some have compassion, making a distinction, [23] and some save, snatching them out of the fire with fear, hating even the clothing stained by the flesh. [24] Now to him who is able to keep them from stumbling, and to present you faultless before the presence of his glory in great joy, [25] to God our Savior, who alone is wise, be glory and majesty, dominion and power, both now and forever. Amen.

What insight if any does this Scripture give you about what it looks like to *walk in the Spirit*?

To *walk in the Spirit* we need to know the Spirit, Jesus, the Word. What words are used in this text to remind you of who Jesus/Spirit/God is?

What distractions are noted herein (if any) that might hinder someone from *walking in the Spirit*?

How can I apply this instruction to my life going forward, in my daily *walk in the Spirit*?

#146 1 Corinthians 14:12-17 ^(NASB)

So also you, since you are zealous of spiritual *gifts*, seek to abound for the edification of the church. [13] Therefore let one who speaks in a tongue pray that he may interpret. [14] For if I pray in a tongue, my spirit prays, but my mind is unfruitful. [15] What is *the outcome* then? I will pray with the spirit and I will pray with the mind also; I will sing with the spirit and I will sing with the mind also. [16] Otherwise if you bless in the spirit *only*, how will the one who fills the place of the ungifted say the "Amen" at your giving of thanks, since he does not know what you are saying? [17] For you are giving thanks well enough, but the other person is not edified.

What insight if any does this Scripture give you about what it looks like to *walk in the Spirit*?

To *walk in the Spirit* we need to know the Spirit, Jesus, the Word. What words are used in this text to remind you of who Jesus/Spirit/God is?

What distractions are noted herein (if any) that might hinder someone from *walking in the Spirit*?

How can I apply this instruction to my life going forward, in my daily *walk in the Spirit*?

#147 Romans 15:30-33

Now I beg you, brothers, by our Lord Jesus Christ and by the love of the Spirit, that you strive together with me in your prayers to God for me, [31] that I may be delivered from those who are disobedient in Judea, and that my service which I have for Jerusalem may be acceptable to the saints, [32] that I may come to you in joy through the will of God, and together with you, find rest. [33] Now the God of peace be with you all. Amen.

What insight if any does this Scripture give you about what it looks like to *walk in the Spirit*?

To *walk in the Spirit* we need to know the Spirit, Jesus, the Word. What words are used in this text to remind you of who Jesus/Spirit/God is?

What distractions are noted herein (if any) that might hinder someone from *walking in the Spirit*?

How can I apply this instruction to my life going forward, in my daily *walk in the Spirit*?

#148 Acts 4:29-31

"Now, Lord, look at their threats, and grant to your servants to speak your word with all boldness, [30] while you stretch out your hand to heal; and that signs and wonders may be done through the name of your holy Servant Jesus." [31] When they had prayed, the place was shaken where they were gathered together. They were all filled with the Holy Spirit, and they spoke the word of God with boldness.

What insight if any does this Scripture give you about what it looks like to *walk in the Spirit*?

To *walk in the Spirit* we need to know the Spirit, Jesus, the Word. What words are used in this text to remind you of who Jesus/Spirit/God is?

What distractions are noted herein (if any) that might hinder someone from *walking in the Spirit*?

How can I apply this instruction to my life going forward, in my daily *walk in the Spirit*?

#149 <u>Romans 5:1-5</u>

Being therefore <u>justified by faith</u>, we have <u>peace</u> with God through our Lord Jesus Christ; [2] through whom we also have our access by <u>faith</u> into this <u>grace</u> in which we stand. We <u>rejoice in hope</u> of the glory of God. [3] Not only this, but we also <u>rejoice in our sufferings</u>, knowing that suffering produces <u>perseverance</u>; [4] and perseverance, proven <u>character</u>; and proven character, hope: [5] and <u>hope</u> doesn't disappoint us, because <u>God's love</u> has been poured into our hearts <u>through the Holy Spirit</u> who was given to us.

What insight if any does this Scripture give you about what it looks like to *walk in the Spirit*?

To *walk in the Spirit* we need to know the Spirit, Jesus, the Word. What words are used in this text to remind you of who Jesus/Spirit/God is?

What distractions are noted herein (if any) that might hinder someone from *walking in the Spirit*?

How can I apply this instruction to my life going forward, in my daily *walk in the Spirit*?

113

#150 1 Peter 4:12-15

Beloved, don't be astonished at the fiery trial which has come upon you to test you, as though a strange thing happened to you. [13] But because you are partakers of Christ's sufferings, rejoice, that at the revelation of his glory you also may rejoice with exceeding joy. [14] If you are insulted for the name of Christ, you are blessed; because the Spirit of glory and of God rests on you. On their part he is blasphemed, but on your part he is glorified. [15] For let none of you suffer as a murderer, or a thief, or an evil doer, or a meddler in other men's matters. [16] But if one of you suffers for being a Christian, let him not be ashamed; but let him glorify God in this matter.

What insight if any does this Scripture give you about what it looks like to *walk in the Spirit*?

To *walk in the Spirit* we need to know the Spirit, Jesus, the Word. What words are used in this text to remind you of who Jesus/Spirit/God is?

What distractions are noted herein (if any) that might hinder someone from *walking in the Spirit*?

How can I apply this instruction to my life going forward, in my daily *walk in the Spirit*?

#151 Ephesians 4:25-32

Therefore putting away falsehood, speak truth each one with his neighbor. For we are members of one another. [26] "Be angry, and don't sin." Psalm 4:4 Don't let the sun go down on your wrath, [27] and don't give place to the devil. [28] Let him who stole steal no more; but rather let him labor, producing with his hands something that is good, that he may have something to give to him who has need. [29] Let no corrupt speech proceed out of your mouth, but only what is good for building others up as the need may be, that it may give grace to those who hear. [30] Don't grieve the Holy Spirit of God, in whom you were sealed for the day of redemption. [31] Let all bitterness, wrath, anger, outcry, and slander be put away from you, with all malice. [32] And be kind to one another, tender hearted, forgiving each other, just as God also in Christ forgave you.

What insight if any does this Scripture give you about what it looks like to *walk in the Spirit*?

To *walk in the Spirit* we need to know the Spirit, Jesus, the Word. What words are used in this text to remind you of who Jesus/Spirit/God is?

What distractions are noted herein (if any) that might hinder someone from *walking in the Spirit*?

How can I apply this instruction to my life going forward, in my daily *walk in the Spirit*?

#152 <u>1 Corinthians 13:4-7</u> ^(NKJV)

<u>Love suffers long *and* is kind; love does not envy; love does not parade itself, is not puffed up; ⁵ does not behave rudely, does not seek its own, is not provoked, thinks no evil; ⁶ does not rejoice in iniquity, but rejoices in the truth; ⁷ bears all things, believes all things, hopes all things, endures all things.</u>

What insight if any does this Scripture give you about what it looks like to *walk in the Spirit*?

To *walk in the Spirit* we need to know the Spirit, Jesus, the Word. What words are used in this text to remind you of who Jesus/Spirit/God is?

What distractions are noted herein (if any) that might hinder someone from *walking in the Spirit*?

How can I apply this instruction to my life going forward, in my daily *walk in the Spirit*?

#153 Ezekiel 36:26-28

I will also give you a new heart, and I will put a new spirit within you. I will take away the stony heart out of your flesh, and I will give you a heart of flesh. [27] I will put my Spirit within you, and cause you to walk in my statutes. You will keep my ordinances and do them. [28] You will dwell in the land that I gave to your fathers. You will be my people, and I will be your God.

What insight if any does this Scripture give you about what it looks like to *walk in the Spirit*?

WALK **in the** SPIRIT

To *walk in the Spirit* we need to know the Spirit, Jesus, the Word. What words are used in this text to remind you of who Jesus/Spirit/God is?

What distractions are noted herein (if any) that might hinder someone from *walking in the Spirit*?

How can I apply this instruction to my life going forward, in my daily *walk in the Spirit*?

122

Appendix A - Small Group Facilitation Guide

A well-prepared small group facilitator reads and documents his/her own responses to each teaching *beforehand*. Being prepared will make the facilitation process more enjoyable for all. Facilitation is also best when we ***do*** what we believe Jesus was telling us to do, in advance of the meeting. See Appendix B for a sample of how one might answer the questions, particularly the first time.

When we facilitate small groups, it's best to lead with our *heart*. Facilitators can get their heart ready before the meeting by praying, reading the Word, worshipping. And we can tell if we are in the Spirit by the fruit: peace, joy, love, patience, kindness, gentleness, self-control, faithfulness and goodness.

We should try to avoid showing favoritism if we like certain responses. Rather give a hearty "thank you" to each person after he/she shares. Overall, be patient with yourself and others during the learning process. Remember, one plants, another waters, but it's God who gives the increase.

The facilitation process:

- o After a bit of fellowship, open in prayer.
- o Read the first couple of paragraphs in the introduction for anyone that is attending for the first time, so that he/she is reminded of the goal of the study.
- o Ask for a volunteer to read the Scripture. If no takers, read it yourself.
- o Read the first discussion question, "What insight if any does this Scripture give you about what it looks like to *walk in the Spirit*?" The questions encourage active participation from each person. At the same time the facilitator is careful to avoid any one individual from dominating the discussion, or another from hiding. Before going to the next question, ask if anyone has any other thoughts or insights.

The facilitation process (continued):

- o Repeat for next questions.
- o After you read the last question, give everyone a few minutes to write their answers in their books. Afterwards, go around the room and ask *each individual* to share what he/she wrote.
- o Ask for a volunteer to close in prayer.

After a few meetings individuals should become accustomed to the facilitation process, so that almost anyone in the group could facilitate the meeting.

Appendix A – Sample Answers

John 15:1-5 ^(NASB)

"I am the true vine, and My Father is the vinedresser. ² Every branch in Me that does not bear fruit, He takes away; and every *branch* that bears fruit, He prunes it so that it may bear more fruit. ³ You are already clean because of the word which I have spoken to you. ⁴ Abide in Me, and I in you. As the branch cannot bear fruit of itself unless it abides in the vine, so neither *can* you unless you abide in Me. ⁵ I am the vine, you are the branches; he who abides in Me and I in him, he bears much fruit, for apart from Me you can do nothing.

What insight if any does this Scripture give you about what it looks like to *walk in the Spirit*?

- We are bearing fruit because we abide in Him, and <u>Him in us</u>
- We can't bear fruit on our own
- We are constantly getting pruned (perhaps things of the flesh)
- We are cleansed from sin because of Christ
- We abide in the vine, in Christ
- We're never apart from Him, never alone

To *walk in the Spirit* we need to know the Spirit, Jesus, the Word. What words are used in this text to remind you of who Jesus/Spirit/God is?

- Jesus is the true vine
- The Father is the vinedresser
- The Father invests His time in me and prunes me
- Jesus has made me clean

125

- Jesus abides in me
- The One I abide in

What distractions are noted herein (if any) that might hinder someone from *walking in the Spirit*?

- I try to do things in the flesh and in my own strength. I cannot bear fruit, unless I abide in Him, and Him in me; apart from Him I can do nothing
- I don't stay clean (free from flesh, world, devil)
- I don't abide in Him and in His Word, and therefore are more interesting in things of the world and flesh

How can I apply this instruction to my life going forward, in my daily *walk in the Spirit*?

- I want to learn more about abiding in Him and in His love.
- I want to bear much fruit with Him in me.
- I want to follow Him, be led by the Spirit
- And although I can do nothing on my own, with God, nothing is impossible!

More Bible studies

The following are some other Bible studies similar to "WALK in the SPIRIT" which are all part of the IN HIM series: abide IN Him, and Him IN us… the Christian walk:

What does it mean to be a Follower *(disciple)* of Jesus Christ today? How do we *follow Jesus* according to the Gospels? Did Jesus have any expectations of His *followers*? Who is Jesus and why did He come? Learn from the Master Himself in *All the times Jesus said 'I am.'*

> Follow JESUS – Part 1 (1-50)
> Follow JESUS - Part 2 (51-83)
> All the times JESUS said I AM (84-147)

How do we Abide in Him and His Words in us? Jesus said, *"If you abide in Me, and My words abide in you, you will ask what you desire, and it shall be done for you. By this My Father is glorified, that you bear much fruit; so you will be My disciples."* How do we abide in Him and His words in us?

> Abide IN the WORD and the WORD IN YOU (1-59)
> DO the WORD (coming soon)
> PREACH the WORD (coming soon)

What and Who is the Truth? What did Jesus mean when He said, *"you shall know the truth, and the truth shall make you free?"* And the letter of 3 John 1:4 reads, *"I have no greater joy than to hear about my children walking in truth."*

> Know the TRUTH (1-45)
> Walk IN the TRUTH (46-86)

How do we live and walk in the Spirit (and not the flesh)?
What does Scripture tell us about the relationship between the Spirit
and our flesh/soul? What does it mean to crucify the flesh? Galatians
5:25 reads, *"If we live in the Spirit, let us also walk in the Spirit."*
What's the difference between *living* in the Spirit and *walking* in the
Spirit?

> Discern SPIRIT and Flesh (1-24)
> Crucify the FLESH (25-58)
> Live IN the SPIRIT (59-95)
> Walk IN the SPIRIT (96-153)

Why is it important that Jesus abide IN US? Jesus said, "He
who abides in Me and I in him, he bears much fruit." 1 John 4:16 reads,
"the one who abides in love abides in God, and God abides in him."
What Scriptures provide insight into Jesus and the Spirit abiding IN
US?

> JESUS Abiding IN YOU (1-36)
> The SPIRIT of GOD IN YOU (37-70)
> Abide IN JESUS and IN HIS LOVE (71-129)

What is Walking and Abiding IN the Light? 1 John 2 reads,
"He who loves his brother abides in the Light." What does it mean to
abide in the Light? Who is the Light? Isaiah 2 reads, "O house of
Jacob, come, let us walk in the light of the Lord." How do we walk in
the Light of the Lord?

> Abide IN the LIGHT (1-33)
> Walk IN the LIGHT (34-64)

When does Eternal Life and New Life IN Christ begin?
Jesus is the source of life and eternal life. When does eternal life in

Christ Jesus begin? What is life in Christ Jesus? What does Romans 6:4 mean by, "walk in newness of life?"

Life IN CHRIST JESUS (1-40)
Walk IN the NEWNESS of LIFE (41-86)

What has Christ Set us Free from? Whom the Son set free is free indeed. Free from what and to what?

The Call to Freedom IN CHRIST (1-50)

What happens when we put our Trust and Hope in Him? Jeremiah 17:7 reads, "Blessed *is* the man who trusts in the Lord, and whose hope is the Lord." We can have a hope for a future, a hope to enter His rest, a hope that does not disappoint.

Hope IN the LORD (1-57)

Made in the USA
Monee, IL
14 April 2022